22754

IMMIGRATION FROM THE DOMINICAN REPUBLIC

Kimberly A. Rinker

THE CHANGING
Face of North America:
IMMIGRATION SINCE 1965

Asylees

Chinese Immigration

Cuban Immigration

Deported Aliens

Filipino Immigration

Haitian Immigration

Immigration from Central America

Immigration from the Dominican Republic

Immigration from the Former Yugoslavia

Immigration from the Middle East

Immigration from South America

Indian Immigration

Korean Immigration

Mexican Immigration

Refugees

Vietnamese Immigration

IMMIGRATION FROM THE DOMINICAN REPUBLIC

Kimberly A. Rinker

MASON CREST PUBLISHERS
PHILADELPHIA

Produced by OTTN Publishing, Stockton, New Jersey

Mason Crest Publishers
370 Reed Road
Broomall, PA 19008
www.masoncrest.com

First printing

1 3 5 7 9 8 6 4 2

Library of Congress Cataloging-in-Publication Data

Rinker, Kimberly A.
  Immigration from the Dominican Republic / Kimberly A. Rinker.
     p. cm. — (The changing face of North America)
Includes bibliographical references and index.
Summary: Surveys immigration from the Dominican Republic to the United States and Canada since the 1960s, as a
result of changes in immigration law.
  ISBN 1-59084-689-3
1. Dominican Americans—History—20th century—Juvenile literature. 2. Dominicans (Dominican Republic)—
Canada—History—20th century—Juvenile literature. 3. Immigrants—United States—History—20th
century—Juvenile literature. 4. Immigrants—Canada—History—20th century—Juvenile literature. 5. Dominican
Republic—Emigration and immigration—History—20th century—Juvenile literature. 6. United States—Emigration
and immigration—History—20th century—Juvenile literature. 7. Canada—Emigration and immigration—
History—20th century—Juvenile literature. [1. Dominican Americans. 2. Dominican Republic—Emigration and
immigration.] I. Title. II. Series.
  E184.D6R56 2004
  304.8'7307293—dc22
                                                                              2003018812

THE **CHANGING**
Face of North America:
IMMIGRATION SINCE 1965

CONTENTS

INTRODUCTION

THE CHANGING FACE OF AMERICA

By Senator Edward M. Kennedy

America is proud of its heritage and history as a nation of immigrants, and my own family is an example. All eight of my great-grandparents were immigrants who left Ireland a century and a half ago, when that land was devastated by the massive famine caused by the potato blight. When I was a young boy, my grandfather used to take me down to the docks in Boston and regale me with stories about the Great Famine and the waves of Irish immigrants who came to America seeking a better life. He talked of how the Irish left their marks in Boston and across the nation, enduring many hardships and harsh discrimination, but also building the railroads, digging the canals, settling the West, and filling the factories of a growing America. According to one well-known saying of the time, "under every railroad tie, an Irishman is buried."

America was the promised land for them, as it has been for so many other immigrants who have found shelter, hope, opportunity, and freedom. Immigrants have always been an indispensable part of our nation. They have contributed immensely to our communities, created new jobs and whole new industries, served in our armed forces, and helped make America the continuing land of promise that it is today.

The inspiring poem by Emma Lazarus, inscribed on the pedestal of the Statue of Liberty in New York Harbor, is America's welcome to all immigrants:

Give me your tired, your poor,
Your huddled masses yearning to breathe free,
The wretched refuse of your teeming shore,
Send these, the homeless, tempest-tossed, to me:
I lift my lamp beside the golden door.

The period since September 11, 2001, has been particularly challenging for immigrants. Since the horrifying terrorist attacks, there has been a resurgence of anti-immigrant attitudes and behavior. We all agree that our borders must be safe and secure. Yet, at the same time, we must safeguard the entry of the millions of persons who come to the United States legally each year as immigrants, visitors, scholars, students, and workers. The "golden door" must stay open. We must recognize that immigration is not the problem—terrorism is. We must identify and isolate the terrorists, and not isolate America.

One of my most important responsibilities in the Senate is the preservation of basic rights and basic fairness in the application of our immigration laws, so that new generations of immigrants in our own time and for all time will have the same opportunity that my great-grandparents had when they arrived in America.

Immigration is beneficial for the United States and for countries throughout the world. It is no coincidence that two hundred years ago, our nations' founders chose *E Pluribus Unum*—"out of many, one"—as America's motto. These words, chosen by Benjamin Franklin, John Adams, and Thomas Jefferson, refer to the ideal that separate colonies can be transformed into one united nation. Today, this ideal has come to apply to individuals as well. Our diversity is our strength. We are a nation of immigrants, and we always will be.

FOREWORD

THE CHANGING FACE OF THE UNITED STATES

Marian L. Smith, historian
U.S. Immigration and Naturalization Service

Americans commonly assume that immigration today is very different than immigration of the past. The immigrants themselves appear to be unlike immigrants of earlier eras. Their language, their dress, their food, and their ways seem strange. At times people fear too many of these new immigrants will destroy the America they know. But has anything really changed? Do new immigrants have any different effect on America than old immigrants a century ago? Is the American fear of too much immigration a new development? Do immigrants really change America more than America changes the immigrants? The very subject of immigration raises many questions.

In the United States, immigration is more than a chapter in a history book. It is a continuous thread that links the present moment to the first settlers on North American shores. From the first colonists' arrival until today, immigrants have been met by Americans who both welcomed and feared them. Immigrant contributions were always welcome—on the farm, in the fields, and in the factories. Welcoming the poor, the persecuted, and the "huddled masses" became an American principle. Beginning with the original Pilgrims' flight from religious persecution in the 1600s, through the Irish migration to escape starvation in the 1800s, to the relocation of Central Americans seeking refuge from civil wars in the 1980s and 1990s, the United States has considered itself a haven for the destitute and the oppressed.

But there was also concern that immigrants would not adopt American ways, habits, or language. Too many immigrants might overwhelm America. If so, the dream of the Founding Fathers for United States government and society would be destroyed. For this reason, throughout American history some have argued that limiting or ending immigration is our patriotic duty. Benjamin Franklin feared there were so many German immigrants in Pennsylvania the Colonial Legislature would begin speaking German. "Progressive" leaders of the early 1900s feared that immigrants who could not read and understand the English language were not only exploited by "big business," but also served as the foundation for "machine politics" that undermined the U.S. Constitution. This theme continues today, usually voiced by those who bear no malice toward immigrants but who want to preserve American ideals.

Have immigrants changed? In colonial days, when most colonists were of English descent, they considered Germans, Swiss, and French immigrants as different. They were not "one of us" because they spoke a different language. Generations later, Americans of German or French descent viewed Polish, Italian, and Russian immigrants as strange. They were not "like us" because they had a different religion, or because they did not come from a tradition of constitutional government. Recently, Americans of Polish or Italian descent have seen Nicaraguan, Pakistani, or Vietnamese immigrants as too different to be included. It has long been said of American immigration that the latest ones to arrive usually want to close the door behind them.

It is important to remember that fear of individual immigrant groups seldom lasted, and always lessened. Benjamin Franklin's anxiety over German immigrants disappeared after those immigrants' sons and daughters helped the nation gain independence in the Revolutionary War. The Irish of the mid-1800s were among the most hated immigrants, but today we all wear green on St. Patrick's Day. While a century ago it was feared that Italian and other Catholic immigrants would vote as directed by the Pope, today that controversy is only a vague memory. Unfortunately, some ethnic groups continue their efforts to earn acceptance. The African

Americans' struggle continues, and some Asian Americans, whose families have been in America for generations, are the victims of current anti-immigrant sentiment.

Time changes both immigrants and America. Each wave of new immigrants, with their strange language and habits, eventually grows old and passes away. Their American-born children speak English. The immigrants' grandchildren are completely American. The strange foods of their ancestors—spaghetti, baklava, hummus, or tofu—become common in any American restaurant or grocery store. Much of what the immigrants brought to these shores is lost, principally their language. And what is gained becomes as American as St. Patrick's Day, Hanukkah, or Cinco de Mayo, and we forget that it was once something foreign.

Recent immigrants are all around us. They come from every corner of the earth to join in the American Dream. They will continue to help make the American Dream a reality, just as all the immigrants who came before them have done.

FOREWORD

THE CHANGING FACE OF CANADA

Peter A. Hammerschmidt
First Secretary, Permanent Mission of Canada to the United Nations

Throughout Canada's history, immigration has shaped and defined the very character of Canadian society. The migration of peoples from every part of the world into Canada has profoundly changed the way we look, speak, eat, and live. Through close and distant relatives who left their lands in search of a better life, all Canadians have links to immigrant pasts. We are a nation built by and of immigrants.

Two parallel forces have shaped the history of Canadian immigration. The enormous diversity of Canada's immigrant population is the most obvious. In the beginning came the enterprising settlers of the "New World," the French and English colonists. Soon after came the Scottish, Irish, and Northern and Central European farmers of the 1700s and 1800s. As the country expanded westward during the mid-1800s, migrant workers began arriving from China, Japan, and other Asian countries. And the turbulent twentieth century brought an even greater variety of immigrants to Canada, from the Caribbean, Africa, India, and Southeast Asia.

So while English- and French-Canadians are the largest ethnic groups in the country today, neither group alone represents a majority of the population. A large and vibrant multicultural mix makes up the rest, particularly in Canada's major cities. Toronto, Vancouver, and Montreal alone are home to people from over 200 ethnic groups!

Less obvious but equally important in the evolution of Canadian immigration has been hope. The promise of a better life lured Europeans and Americans seeking cheap (sometimes even free) farmland. Thousands of Scots and Irish arrived to escape grinding poverty and starvation. Others came for freedom, to escape religious and political persecution. Canada has long been a haven to the world's dispossessed and disenfranchised—Dutch and German farmers cast out for their religious beliefs, black slaves fleeing the United States, and political refugees of despotic regimes in Europe, Africa, Asia, and South America.

The two forces of diversity and hope, so central to Canada's past, also shaped the modern era of Canadian immigration. Following the Second World War, Canada drew heavily on these influences to forge trailblazing immigration initiatives.

The catalyst for change was the adoption of the Canadian Bill of Rights in 1960. Recognizing its growing diversity and Canadians' changing attitudes towards racism, the government passed a federal statute barring discrimination on the grounds of race, national origin, color, religion, or sex. Effectively rejecting the discriminatory elements in Canadian immigration policy, the Bill of Rights forced the introduction of a new policy in 1962. The focus of immigration abruptly switched from national origin to the individual's potential contribution to Canadian society. The door to Canada was now open to every corner of the world.

Welcoming those seeking new hopes in a new land has also been a feature of Canadian immigration in the modern era. The focus on economic immigration has increased along with Canada's steadily growing economy, but political immigration has also been encouraged. Since 1945, Canada has admitted tens of thousands of displaced persons, including Jewish Holocaust survivors, victims of Soviet crackdowns in Hungary and Czechoslovakia, and refugees from political upheaval in Uganda, Chile, and Vietnam.

Prior to 1978, however, these political refugees were admitted as an exception to normal immigration procedures. That year, Canada

revamped its refugee policy with a new Immigration Act that explicit-
ly affirmed Canada's commitment to the resettlement of refugees
from oppression. Today, the admission of refugees remains a central
part of Canadian immigration law and regulations.

Amendments to economic and political immigration policy
continued during the 1980s and 1990s, refining further the bold
steps taken during the modern era. Together, these initiatives have
turned Canada into one of the world's few truly multicultural states.

Unlike the process of assimilation into a "melting pot" of cultures,
immigrants to Canada are more likely to retain their cultural identity,
beliefs, and practices. This is the source of some of Canada's
greatest strengths as a society. And as a truly multicultural nation,
diversity is not seen as a threat to Canadian identity. Quite the
contrary—diversity *is* Canadian identity.

1 LEAVING THE CARIBBEAN

Immigrants to North America from the Dominican Republic, which shares a large island with Haiti in the Caribbean Sea, make up one of the largest groups immigrating from the Caribbean. Sparked by the hopes of a better life in a new land, Dominicans began migrating to the United States and Canada in the latter half of the 20th century. The 2000 U.S. Census recorded over 692,000 Dominican-born people in the country, and the 2001 Canadian census recorded over 5,000 Dominican-born residents.

The small country of the Dominican Republic (which is the size of the state of Georgia) and its 8.7 million people have a strong immigration relationship with North America. Since the 1960s, migration to the United States has been relatively high compared to that of most other countries. Impoverished conditions, high unemployment, and a poor educational system in the Dominican Republic have prompted many Dominicans with average or below-average incomes to consider moving to the United States. A large percentage of Dominicans have resettled in New York City.

In 2002, the Dominican Republic ranked ninth among countries sending legal immigrants to the United States, with a total for that year of over 22,500. Canada is also a place to settle for Dominican immigrants, though it is not nearly

◀ These girls may one day join the thousands of Dominicans who annually cross the Caribbean waters to resettle in North America. In 2002, the Dominican Republic ranked ninth among countries sending legal immigrants to the United States.

as popular as the United States. Dominican immigrants to Canada generally have resettled in the three major cities of Montreal, Ottawa, and Toronto.

The majority of Dominican immigrants who move to North America reunite with family members already established there. Most of these immigrants hope that by receiving the higher wages available in North America, they will help improve the lives of family and friends by sending home money (payments called "remittances"). Through the 19th century and into the 1960s, many Dominicans immigrated to escape the homeland's political turmoil. Eventually, the years of political unrest took a great toll on the Dominican economy, prompting even more migration to North America during the 1980s and 1990s.

Historically, most of the Dominicans who have immigrated to North America have represented the upper and middle classes, although in recent years more migrants with lower incomes have arrived. To accomplish the move, which is made via boat or plane, Dominicans must procure the proper resources. Family connections and money are vital to an immigrant's journey, especially in terms of securing a resident visa. To accomplish this, most immigrants enter the United States or Canada under the sponsorship of relatives who are already U.S. citizens or legal immigrants and have accumulated some money.

Choosing the United States

There are a number of reasons why Dominicans prefer settling in the United States to settling in Canada. First—and the most obvious reason—the United States is physically closer to the Dominican Republic. Santo Domingo, the Dominican Republic's capital and largest city, is only 886 miles (1,426 kilometers) south of Key West, Florida.

Second, the United States and the Dominican Republic enjoy long-lasting economic ties. Because the Dominican Republic is second only to Cuba in terms of population size and land area, the United States has always showed interest in developments there. Likewise, the Dominican Republic has supported the international policies of the United States, and has cooperated with its government in monitoring illegal drug trafficking and people smuggling. The United States receives 65 percent of Dominican

A street vendor in the Dominican capital of Santo Domingo sells American-made cigarettes and other products. The United States' reputation as a popular immigrant destination is bolstered by the strong economic ties between the Dominican Republic and its much wealthier neighbor.

exports, which primarily consist of coffee, sugar, and tobacco. Trade between the two nations has always been strong, and U.S.–based manufacturers of shoes, clothing, and electronics account for a large share of private investment within the Dominican Republic.

Third, the Dominican people have been heavily influenced by American culture for several decades. In the larger Dominican cities such as Santo Domingo or San

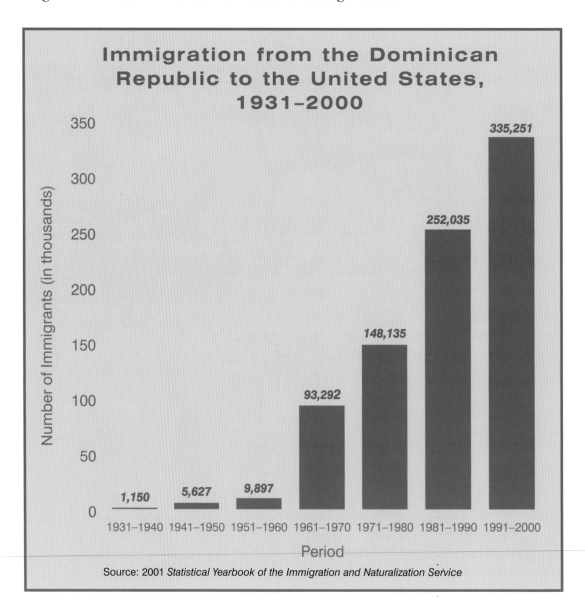

Immigration from the Dominican Republic to the United States, 1931–2000

Source: 2001 *Statistical Yearbook of the Immigration and Naturalization Service*

Pedro de Macorís, many of the streets are named after prominent American figures like John F. Kennedy and Abraham Lincoln. Baseball, television, and films are some of the popular American traditions that the Dominicans have adopted.

The major center of Dominican life in North America is New York City. According to 2000 U.S. Census figures, Dominicans are the second-largest group of Hispanics or Latinos—next to Puerto Ricans—living in New York City. Nearly 70 percent of all Dominican immigrants reside in the state of New York (the majority living in New York City), while the remainder can be found primarily in New Jersey, Florida, Massachusetts, Rhode Island, Pennsylvania, Connecticut, and Washington, D.C. Over 10 percent of the children enrolled in New York City's public school system are Dominicans or Dominican Americans (those born in the United States to Dominican immigrant parents). Dominicans have formed their own neighborhoods in New York City, the most established of which are in Queens, the South Bronx, Brooklyn, and on the Upper and Lower East Side of Manhattan. In neighboring New Jersey, small contingents reside in Hoboken, Newark, Jersey City, and Union City.

Immigrating to Canada

The pattern of Dominican immigration to Canada has been consistent with general immigration patterns from the Caribbean region. Historically, there have been lower numbers of immigrants from the Caribbean and Latin America to Canada than those immigrating from Europe. In recent years, those numbers have also been low relative to the immigrant numbers from Asian countries like China, India, Pakistan, and South Korea. Dominican migration to the country was very sparse at the beginning of the 20th century. By the mid-1950s and through the latter half of the century, Dominican professionals began venturing in small groups to Canada for training in fields such as medicine and engineering.

Although Canada is one of the world's leading countries in receiving immigrants, with newcomers accounting for 17 percent of the country's population, Dominicans comprise only a small segment of the immigrant population. During the past 40 years Canada has proven a more popular place to settle for the other national group of Hispaniola, the Haitians, as well as for Jamaicans and Trinidadians.

From 1996 to 2001, only 1,150 Dominicans immigrated to Canada. The 2001 census reported that Dominicans made up less than 1 percent of the country's 5.4 million foreign-born. The few Dominicans who do immigrate to Canada, however, have a high success rate. Four out of five become Canadian citizens, and they also tend to migrate as complete families rather than as individuals. As a result of the passing of the Immigration and Refugee Protection Act (IRPA) in June 2002, government agencies anticipate that Dominican immigrants, particularly those sponsored by family members, should be processed more efficiently. This reform could result in a higher rate of Dominican immigration to Canada.

The economic relationship between Canada and the Dominican Republic, and Canada's interest in the island country's development since the middle of the 20th century, perhaps has influenced some of the migration of recent decades. The Dominican Republic is one of Canada's main investment markets in the Caribbean, with mining, tourism, and communications as prominent services and industries. Canada is also the second-largest banking investor in the Dominican Republic, with the Bank of Nova Scotia and the Royal Bank of Canada as the country's main banks. The economic ties between Canada and the Dominican Republic have continued to improve in recent years. The countries' leaders met in late 2002 and again in 2003 to discuss writing a bilateral free-trade agreement.

Religious organizations have also played a moderate role in helping spur migration to Canada. Orders of the Congregation du Sacre Coeur and the Scarboro Missionary Fathers established themselves in the Dominican Republic in the 1940s. These groups, along with several congregations of Canadian nuns, introduced their land and culture to native Dominicans during that period.

2

THE HOMELAND AND ITS PEOPLE

Columbus landed on Hispaniola during his maiden voyage in 1492. At that time the Taino Indians were the sole inhabitants of the island, which they called Quisqueya. These indigenous inhabitants, who spoke the Arawak language, were estimated to number one million people when Columbus first encountered them. The explorer and the Tainos got along well, but the colonists who came after Columbus certainly did not live peacefully with the natives. Over the next 50 years, fighting and disease reduced the Taino population to a mere 500 people.

Columbus dubbed the island La Española in honor of Spain, and named his son Diego as the country's first viceroy. For a period of 500 years, beginning with Diego Columbus's rule, the inhabitants of Hispaniola were victims of poor leadership and great poverty. Only as recently as the final decade of the 20th century did democracy emerge in this island nation.

The Europeans began importing African slaves to the island as early as 1503, and by the 1800s, the Dominican population numbered about 150,000 people, with 40,000 of Spanish descent, 40,000 African slaves, and the rest a combination of freed blacks and mulattoes. By the latter part of the 20th century, 16 percent of the Dominican population was white, 11 percent was black, and the rest was mulatto.

◀ This painting depicts the landing of Christopher Columbus and his party on Hispaniola in 1492. The settlers who came after Columbus initiated a long history of fighting on the island, of which the present-day Dominican Republic shares the eastern two-thirds.

A monument to Juan Pablo Duarte, hero for Dominican independence, stands in Santo Domingo. In 1844 Duarte led the revolution to remove Haitian occupiers from the eastern side of the island and establish an autonomous Dominican Republic.

Colonization and Revolt

France took control of the island colony in 1795, but then relinquished it to the Haitians in 1801, under the leadership of former slave Toussaint L'Ouverture. The successor to L'Ouverture, General Jean-Jacques Dessalines, proclaimed the entire colony an independent country in January 1804.

Spain took back control of the country in 1814, but was overthrown again eight years later by the Haitians, who maintained control of the island until 1844. Later that same year, Juan Pablo Duarte, recognized as the hero of Dominican independence, established the Dominican Republic after removing the Haitians. However, after another series of attacks by the neighboring Haitians, the Dominicans later decided to ask for

Spain's military assistance. In exchange for this protection, the country became a province of Spain, an agreement that lasted from 1861 to 1865.

Buenaventura Báez assumed the presidency in 1865 and began changing the Dominican constitution to allot himself more power. He also initiated measures that favored his political allies and the Dominican aristocrats. Báez was forced to resign in 1866, and the next two years were a period of political turmoil for Dominicans. He returned and resumed his presidency in 1868. After he was forced out of office in 1874, he returned once again the following year to set up another regime that was corrupt and oppressive. His reign finally came to an end in 1886.

Ulises Heureaux, who took over after Báez, was a tyrant whose rule in the Dominican Republic saw economic depression and domestic unrest. He was assassinated in

U.S. Marines man patrol boats on the Ozama River in Santo Domingo, 1919. During a period of internal conflict between 1916 and 1924, the U.S. military remained on the island to keep the peace. It returned in 1965 after the outbreak of another civil war.

1899, and the resulting turmoil eventually led to the U.S. government's decision to step in and take over the collection of custom duties in 1905, an arrangement that lasted until 1940.

To maintain order and prevent rebellions, the United States sent marines into the country in 1916 and remained there until 1924. Following the departure of the U.S. military, the Dominican army reemerged as the country's strongest political force, and in 1930 a dictatorship was established under Rafael Trujillo, a former sergeant in the Dominican army. Under the dictator, export industries expanded and the infrastructure was improved. However, the country was certainly not a democracy, as

Where Is Columbus Buried?

Where is the final resting place of Christopher Columbus? Both Spain and the Dominican Republic claim that honor, and their disagreement involves a series of events shrouded in the mists of the past.

Each side agrees on certain basic facts. After his death in Valladolid, Spain, in 1506, Columbus's body was buried in a monastery there. Three years later, the admiral's remains were dug up and reburied in another monastery in Seville. When Columbus's oldest son, Diego, died in 1526, Diego's body was buried beside that of his father. Soon, though, Diego's widow petitioned that the remains of father and son be taken to the island of Hispaniola for reburial—as had been Christopher Columbus's wish. In 1537 the royal court of Spain finally granted the request. The remains of Christopher and Diego Columbus were dug up and placed on a ship bound for the Caribbean. Upon arrival on Hispaniola, the two sets of bones were buried in Santo Domingo's cathedral, the father's under the right side of the altar, the son's under the left.

In 1795, however, Spanish authorities ordered Christopher Columbus's remains dug up because they didn't want them to fall into the hands of the French, to whom Spain was ceding its colony of Santo Domingo. The bones were moved to the Spanish colony of Cuba and reburied in the cathedral in Havana. But at the end of the 19th century, in the midst of the Spanish-American War, those remains were dug up yet again, shipped to Spain, and reburied in the cathedral of Seville.

leaders tortured and murdered political enemies, and Trujillo continued to siphon government money for his family. In *A Brief History of the Caribbean,* author Jan Rogozinski estimated the Trujillo fortune during those years to total over $500 million. The family's revenue was drawn from the companies it owned, which controlled 60 percent of the nation's assets and workers.

Naval sentries stand guard outside Christopher Columbus' tomb in the Faro a Colón (Columbus Lighthouse) in Santo Domingo.

By that time, though, a mystery had emerged in the Dominican Republic. In 1877, workers restoring the cathedral in Santo Domingo discovered a lead coffin buried under the altar. The inscription on the coffin referred to the "illustrious and distinguished male, Don Cristóbal Colón"—Christopher Columbus's name in Spanish. Might the wrong set of remains—possibly those of Diego Columbus—been dug up in 1795? Dominicans were convinced that's precisely what had happened. But Spaniards insisted that the bones of "the Admiral of the Ocean Seas" rested in the cathedral of Seville.

In October 1992—the 500th anniversary of Columbus's first voyage of discovery, the Dominican Republic moved the remains it claimed were those of the famous explorer from the Cathedral of Santa María la Menor to a new monument. The cross-shaped Faro a Colón (Columbus Lighthouse) stands on the Avenida España in Santo Domingo. The imposing memorial is more than a tourist attraction, however. For the Dominican Republic, being the final resting place of history's most famous explorer is a matter of national pride—though Christopher Columbus's mortal remains may in fact reside in Seville or even, as some historians have suggested, in Cuba.

During Trujillo's dictatorship, the government limited emigration and supported an increase in child bearing in the Dominican Republic. Trujillo believed that an increase in population would help support his dictatorship and strengthen the country by securing a larger labor force for the future. His regime offered incentives to large families and to European immigrants who wanted to settle in the Dominican Republic and raise families.

As is the fate of many dictators, Trujillo's rule came to a violent end with his assassination in 1961. Trujillo's death marked the beginning of a new era in Dominican history. Joaquín Balaguer, a former cohort of Trujillo, tried to take over the government after his friend was killed, but he was forced to leave the country in 1962. The country remained in turmoil until April 1965, when U.S. President Lyndon Johnson dispatched marines to restore order.

A New Era of Stability

Balaguer returned to the Dominican Republic and was elected to office in 1966. U.S. troops and other foreign military forces withdrew as Balaguer set up political and economical reforms to stabilize the country.

After serving three terms, Balaguer conceded his presidency in 1978 to Antonio Guzmán, although only after the military's attempt to steal the election for Balaguer was met with both domestic and international outcry, including the intervention of U.S. President Jimmy Carter. After the election of Salvador Jorge Blanco as president in 1982, Guzmán killed himself after charges of corruption in his administration surfaced. In 1986, Balaguer was reelected to a fourth term and stayed in office until 1996, the year the election was won by Leonel Fernández, a lawyer raised in New York City and who practiced in the United States.

During his tenure as president, Fernández was praised for improving relations with other Caribbean countries, but was criticized for not sufficiently fighting corruption or working to alleviate poverty in the Dominican Republic. Rafael Hipolito Mejia, an agricultural economist with a colorful personality, was elected president in August 2000, and in 2001 used the nation's army to fight rising crime in major Dominican cities.

Many people believe the Dominican government is still guilty of committing human rights violations. According to the U.S. State Department's 2002 human rights report on the country, although the Dominican constitution recognizes the autonomy of the government's branches, "interference from outside forces, including the executive branch, remained a problem." The State Department also raised many questions about the way the government treats Dominican citizens, calling its human rights record "poor." The report included descriptions of poor prison conditions, killings by police officials, and the mistreatment of Haitian migrants.

A Struggling Economy

The State Department report also described the Dominican Republic's economic conditions, which, along with political unrest, has influenced the decisions of many citizens to emigrate. The report estimated that 16 percent of the population was unemployed, and that "income distribution in the country was highly skewed."

Prior to 1950 the country's economy was primarily agricultural. But since that year, during which an estimated 75 percent of the people lived in rural areas, more and more Dominicans have left behind the farming life. The expansion of small villages and towns began in the late 1950s, and in succeeding decades growth remained slow but steady, continuing into the 21st century.

Baseball Recruiting in the Dominican Republic

Recruiting young athletes for a career in major league baseball has become a controversial issue in the Dominican Republic. This controversy primarily stems from the age of the recruits—many of whom are truly youngsters, as young as nine or ten years old when they are first contacted by a *buscone* (recruiter). Increased demand for new talent has given rise to *buscones*, whom some people see as a troubling element of the Dominican baseball industry.

Buscones are streetwise, self-appointed agents who train and groom young hopefuls. Some are legitimate coaches who simply encourage and develop talents. Others try to take advantage of the young athletes by signing them to contracts that do not provide nearly as much as the players deserve.

There are 25 major league teams that have set up programs in the Dominican Republic for recruiting and developing potential players. The most extensive is the Los Angeles Dodgers' facility, Campo Las Palmas, which has players in training six days a week. Baseball fields are scattered throughout the country, which has its own professional league. Over one dozen major league baseball academies exist in the town of Campo Las Palmas, which also boasts of former hometown players like Sammy Sosa, Tony Fernandez, George Bell, Pedro Martinez, and Julio Franco.

As people began moving from the farms into urban areas, manufacturing and service sectors grew in the Dominican Republic, which in turn led to increased trade with other nations. Santo Domingo saw its population double every decade between 1920 and 1970. Santiago de los Caballeros, the nation's second-largest city, and La Romana, the third-largest city, experienced tremendous population growth during the same period. By this point, there were more people in Dominican cities than there were jobs, pushing unemployed Dominicans to seek work elsewhere. Often the first course of action was to resettle in North America.

Dominicans were no strangers to hard labor, as most

worked six days a week in the homeland. Both men and woman were part of the labor force, with 84 percent of the women contributing to the family's earnings. In rural communities, a traditional work group known as a junta was and still is commonplace among Dominicans. Friends, relatives, and neighbors often gather at one farmer's house for a day's work, and are paid by returning the favor or in small piece rates.

While the international market of the Dominican Republic experienced positive growth after 1965, domestic growth was very slow. During the 1960s and 1970s, internal changes promised to diversify the economy and

A Dominican rolls cigars in the Leon Jimenez Cigar Factory in Santiago, the Dominican Republic's second-largest city. Many Dominicans work long and hard hours in factories, both on the island and as immigrants in North American cities.

stimulate growth, although Dominicans struggled to readjust. Conditions first became extremely dire when sugar prices plummeted and unemployment rose in the 1970s. The tourism industry brought in much of the country's revenue and compensated for the heavy fluctuations of sugar prices, as did increasing remittances from Dominicans in the United States.

Many Dominican leaders have raised concerns about the country's dependence on the U.S. economy, and have pushed for improved trade with other Caribbean countries, with whom the Dominican Republic has often had strained relations. Responding to this push for a more open policy, President Fernández signed the CARICOM/Dominican Republic Free Trade Agreement in 1998. The agreement with CARICOM (Caribbean Community and Common Market) was put into effect in December 2001.

Immigrants to the Dominican Republic

The Dominican Republic has a society and culture that are unique to the Caribbean and the rest of the world. Continual waves of immigration to the Dominican Republic during the 19th century and the 20th century have deeply affected the ethnic composition of the country. After the Europeans and the African slaves first arrived, several other peoples settled on the island. From 1822 through 1844, some 10,000 Methodists living in North America came to the island, picking up free land that was offered by the Haitians in power at the time.

Jewish people from the island of Curaçao settled after 1844 and assimilated quickly, as did immigrants from the Canary Islands, located off the northwest coast of Spain. In the late 1880s a new group of Spanish landowners emerged from Spain's occupation between

1861 and 1865, and a wave of Germans settled in Puerto Plata, investing in the tobacco trade there. The latter half of the 19th century saw a boom in the Dominican sugar industry, which encouraged the arrival of more Cubans and Puerto Ricans migrants, as well as the British, Dutch, and Danish residents of nearby Caribbean islands. They were not well received by the natives at first, but eventually their industriousness made

Two young Dominicans of the town of Cabrera play the country's favorite sport, *pelota* (baseball). Many Dominican teens aspire to play professional baseball in North America and follow in the footsteps of super-stars like Sammy Sosa and Pedro Martinez.

a good impression. These Europeans soon established churches, aid societies, and other religious and cultural organizations.

Middle Eastern immigrants also settled in the Dominican Republic—first arriving in the late 1880s. Palestinian, Syrian, and Lebanese settlers worked hard to establish businesses and win respect from the natives, and they eventually succeeded. Italians arrived shortly after the turn of the century, as did a few immigrants from South America. These people often began life in the Dominican Republic as domestic servants and cooks, but today some of their descendants own hotels and restaurants on the island.

In the 1930s Jews from Germany began to arrive, and Japanese migrants appeared after World War II. By the 1970s and 1980s Chinese newcomers from Taiwan and Hong Kong had become the fastest-growing immigrant group behind the Haitians. Many of the Asians brought large sums of money to set up manufacturing plants in the country's industrial free zones.

Baseball in the Dominican Republic

Professional baseball has had a significant influence on the migration patterns of Dominicans to the United States, a fact attributed to the sport's enormous popularity in both countries. Milton Jamail discusses this phenomenon in an article in *Studies in Latin American Popular Culture*: "Americans may love the game of baseball as much as Dominicans do, but they do not need it as much. In the Dominican Republic, baseball has a place all out of proportion to the normal one of sport in society."

Playing baseball has become a way of life for many young boys in the Dominican Republic. The sport is a source of hope for them and their families seeking to

Sammy Sosa, who grew up in San Pedro de Macorís, has had more 60-home run seasons than any player in baseball history. He has also funded humanitarian projects that have benefited thousands of needy Dominicans.

escape poverty through a major league position in the United States or Canada.

Among the Dominican immigrants who have played major league baseball in North America over the past several decades, one could assemble an impressive all-time team of stars: For pitchers, the team would have

Juan Marichal, pitcher for the San Francisco Giants, was the first Dominican elected to the Baseball Hall of Fame. He is now the Dominican Republic's minister of sports, and has founded a Little League team in the Dominican neighborhood of Washington Heights, New York City.

two of the best ever, Pedro Martinez and Juan Marichal. At catcher, there's Tony Peña, a five-time All-Star. In the infield, Yankees second baseman Alfonso Soriano; MVP shortstop Miguel Tejada; first baseman Julio Franco; and at backup shortstop, four-time Golden Glove Tony Fernandez. An impressive outfield includes slugger Manny Ramirez, All-Star Vladimir Guerrero, and home run–hitting sensation Sammy Sosa.

One of the most famous players in Dominican history, Sammy Sosa hails from the town of San Pedro de Macorís. He grew up in extreme poverty, and after his father died when Sammy was seven, had to work to help support his family. Playing *pelota* (baseball) became Sammy's favorite pastime when he wasn't working. His first glove was made out of milk cartons, his baseball bats were tree branches, and baseballs were old socks. He played for several minor league Dominican teams before signing with the Texas Rangers at age 16, sending $3,300 of his $3,500 signing bonus home to his family. Slow to develop, he was later traded to the Chicago Cubs, where his career took off. In 1997 Sosa signed a four-year, $42-million contract.

For 37 years, no hitter in the major leagues had been able to best Roger Maris' 1961 record of 61 home runs, until Sammy and Mark McGwire of the St. Louis Cardinals both did it in 1998. Sosa hit 66 home runs that season, the most by any Latin American baseball player ever. In 1999 he hit another stunning 63 home runs, becoming the first player to hit more than 60 home runs in two straight years. He is also one of only a select group of players who has hit more than 500 career home runs.

In 2002, Sosa spoke about his long journey toward becoming a U.S. citizen: "You've got to go step by step and it takes about five to seven years after you get your green card. I'm a U.S. resident now. But when I become a U.S. citizen, that will be a very happy day."

The first Dominican elected to the Baseball Hall of Fame was Juan Marichal, who pitched for the San Francisco Giants. Marichal was born in October 1937 in the Dominican town of Laguna Verde. He appeared in nine All-Star Games and won more games than any other pitcher between 1962 and 1965. He retired from baseball in 1975 and now resides in Santo Domingo as the Dominican Republic's minister of sports. In 1997 he established the Juan Marichal Little League team in Washington Heights, a neighborhood in Upper Manhattan.

In 2002, Omar Minaya achieved a landmark for Dominicans in baseball: he began his tenure as the Montreal Expos general manager, the first Latino to ever hold such a position. Minaya played minor league baseball and became a coach before moving up in baseball organizations as a scout and later as an executive.

According to Tim Wendel, author of *The New Face of Baseball*, Latinos represent 20 percent of all major league players, with players from the Dominican Republic representing the highest proportion of the foreign-born. In his book Wendel quotes Pedro Martinez, who has spoken about how important baseball is for Dominicans. "The sport is big in the Dominican Republic because there are no more paths with the same opportunities," Martinez said. "Maybe that makes us hungrier to play. To do well. All I know is that we need this game more than most people do."

Unless they have become citizens, Dominican baseball players in North America have either the status of lawful permanent residence or they have a temporary visa that allows them to work in the United States or Canada. In 2002, as part of the increased scrutiny given to all foreign nationals seeking admission, U.S. and Canadian embassies more closely checked the birth certificates of Dominican baseball players looking to obtain work visas. In years before, many Dominicans lowered their ages on documents to increase their chances of being picked by major league teams.

3 IMMIGRATING TO NORTH AMERICA

Dominican immigration to North America was not regulated until the 20th century. To place the migration history of this group in a larger context, it is helpful to take a brief journey through the periods of U.S. and Canadian immigration.

Immigration to the United States has been characterized by openness punctuated by periods of restriction. During the 17th, 18th, and 19th centuries, immigration was essentially open without restriction, and, at times, immigrants were even recruited to come to America. Between 1783 and 1820, approximately 250,000 immigrants arrived at U.S. shores. Between 1841 and 1860, more than 4 million immigrants came; most were from England, Ireland, and Germany.

Historically, race and ethnicity have played a role in legislation to restrict immigration. The Chinese Exclusion Act of 1882, which was not repealed until 1943, specifically prevented Chinese people from becoming U.S. citizens and did not allow Chinese laborers to immigrate for the next decade. An agreement with Japan in the early 1900s prevented most Japanese immigration to the United States.

Until the 1920s, no numerical restrictions on immigration existed in the United States, although health restrictions applied. The only other significant restrictions came in 1917, when passing a literacy test became a requirement for

◄The Registry Hall on Ellis Island in New York processed millions of immigrants during the late 19th century and first half of the 20th century. The first Dominican immigrants passed through here and settled in New York and other cities.

immigrants. Presidents Cleveland, Taft, and Wilson had vetoed similar measures earlier. In addition, in 1917 a prohibition was added to the law against the immigration of people from Asia (defined as the Asiatic barred zone). While a few of these prohibitions were lifted during World War II, they were not repealed until 1952, and even then Asians were only allowed in under very small annual quotas.

U.S. Immigration Policy from World War I to 1965

During World War I, the federal government required that all travelers to the United States obtain a visa at a U.S. consulate or diplomatic post abroad. As former State Department consular affairs officer C. D. Scully

A Superstar Reaches Out

Like other immigrants, Dominican baseball superstar Sammy Sosa has shared much of what he has made in the United States with relatives in his home country. He has also become part of a tradition of successful Dominicans providing needy people of the homeland with large donations.

Sosa initiated humanitarian efforts in his homeland as soon as his career abroad took off. In 1996 he began assisting U.S. and Dominican agencies that were coordinating with each other to develop a Haemophilus influenza type b (Hib) vaccine. Hib is the leading cause of meningitis and pneumonia and the leading killer of children in developing countries like the Dominican Republic. The high costs of the vaccine generally hindered its widespread use, a problem that big donators like Sosa have sought to help solve. The U.S. Center for Disease Control and Prevention found that partial Hib vaccinations are just as effective as full vaccinations, which cut the costs to about three dollars per vaccine. Through the contributions of Sosa and others, the Dominican Republic became one of the first developing countries to initiate widespread use of the Hib vaccine.

In September 1998, Sosa's generosity was needed again when Hurricane Georges devastated the island nation, leaving more than

points out, by making that requirement permanent Congress, by 1924, established the framework of temporary, or non-immigrant visas (for study, work, or travel), and immigrant visas (for permanent residence). That framework remains in place today.

After World War I, cultural intolerance and bizarre racial theories led to new immigration restrictions. The House Judiciary Committee employed a eugenics consultant, Dr. Harry N. Laughlin, who asserted that certain races were inferior. Another leader of the eugenics movement, Madison Grant, argued that Jews, Italians, and others were inferior because of their supposedly different skull size.

The Immigration Act of 1924, preceded by the Temporary Quota Act of 1921, set new numerical limits

100,000 people without food or shelter. Sosa coordinated with the Red Cross to send 30,000 pounds of rice, 30,000 pounds of beans, and barrels of clean water to the Dominican Republic, and he aided in the reconstruction of damaged houses. That year he also set up the Sammy Sosa Charitable Foundation (SSCF). The organization's mission is to provide quality education and promote health standards for children both in the United States and in the Dominican Republic. SSCF raised more than $700,000 in 1998, and assisted other Latin American countries as well. In addition, that year Sammy also donated 40 computers to children in the Dominican Republic for every home run he hit.

In August 1999 Sosa opened the Sammy Sosa Children's Medical Center for Preventive Medicine in his hometown of San Pedro de Macorís. The center collaborated with the Dominican and U.S. government agencies in order to administer free immunization packages to 100,000 children annually. The vaccinations included those preventing polio, tuberculosis, diphtheria, tetanus, and measles. The San Pedro center and the Dominican government also initiated plans to build similar centers throughout the country.

on immigration based on "national origin." Taking effect in 1929, the 1924 act set annual quotas on immigrants that were specifically designed to keep out southern Europeans, such as Italians and Greeks. Generally no more than 100 people of the proscribed nationalities were permitted to immigrate.

While the new law was rigid, the U.S. Department of State's restrictive interpretation directed consular officers overseas to be even stricter in their application of the "public charge" provision. (A public charge is someone unable to support himself or his family.) As author Laura Fermi wrote, "In response to the new cry for restriction at the beginning of the [Great Depression] . . . the consuls were to interpret very strictly the clause prohibiting admission of aliens 'likely to become public charges; and to deny the visa to an applicant who in their opinion might become a public charge at any time.'"

In the early 1900s, more than one million immigrants a year came to the United States. In 1930—the first year of the national-origin quotas—approximately 241,700 immigrants were admitted. But under the State Department's strict interpretations, only 23,068 immigrants entered during 1933, the smallest total since 1831. Later these restrictions prevented many Jews in Germany and elsewhere in Europe from escaping what would become the Holocaust. At the height of the Holocaust in 1943, the United States admitted fewer than 6,000 refugees.

The Displaced Persons Act of 1948, the nation's first refugee law, allowed many refugees from World War II to settle in the United States. The law put into place policy changes that had already seen immigration rise from 38,119 in 1945 to 108,721 in 1946 (and later to 249,187 in 1950). One-third of those admitted between 1948 and 1951 were Poles, with ethnic Germans forming the second-largest group.

The 1952 Immigration and Nationality Act is best known for its restrictions against those who supported communism or anarchy. However, the bill's other provisions were quite restrictive and were passed over the veto of President Truman. The 1952 act retained the national-origin quota system for the Eastern Hemisphere. The Western Hemisphere continued to operate without a quota and relied on other qualitative factors to limit immigration. Moreover, during that time, the Mexican bracero program, from 1942 to 1964, allowed millions of Mexican agricultural workers to work temporarily in the United States.

President Lyndon Johnson signed the Immigration Act of 1965, inaugurating a new era of immigration. With the passage of the act, many previously excluded foreign groups were able to immigrate to the United States.

The 1952 act set aside half of each national quota to be divided among three preference categories for relatives of U.S. citizens and permanent residents. The other half went to aliens with high education or exceptional abilities. These quotas applied only to those from the Eastern Hemisphere.

A Halt to the National-Origin Quotas

The Immigration and Nationality Act of 1965 became a landmark in immigration legislation by specifically striking the racially based national-origin quotas. It removed the barriers to Asian immigration, which later led to opportunities to immigrate for many Filipinos, Chinese, Koreans, and others. The Western Hemisphere was designated a ceiling of 120,000 immigrants but without a preference system or per country limits. Modifications made in 1978 ultimately combined the

U.S. Attorney General John Ashcroft defends the controversial USA PATRIOT Act in a speech, August 2003. The act, adopted as part of the war on terrorism following the September 2001 attacks, raised concerns about civil liberties.

Western and Eastern Hemispheres into one preference system and one ceiling of 290,000.

The 1965 act built on the existing system—without the national-origin quotas—and gave somewhat more priority to family relationships. It did not completely overturn the existing system but rather carried forward essentially intact the family immigration categories from the 1959 amendments to the Immigration and Nationality Act. Even though the text of the law prior to 1965 indicated that half of the immigration slots were reserved for skilled employment immigration, in practice, Immigration and Naturalization Service (INS) statistics show that 86 percent of the visas issued between 1952 and 1965 went for family immigration.

A number of significant pieces of legislation since 1980 have shaped the current U.S. immigration system. First, the Refugee Act of 1980 removed refugees from the annual world limit and established that the president would set the number of refugees who could be admitted each year after consultations with Congress.

Second, the 1986 Immigration Reform and Control Act (IRCA) introduced sanctions against employers who "knowingly" hired undocumented immigrants (those here illegally). It also provided amnesty for many undocumented immigrants.

Third, the Immigration Act of 1990 increased legal immigration by 40 percent. In particular, the act significantly increased the number of employment-based immigrants (to 140,000), while also boosting family immigration.

Fourth, the 1996 Illegal Immigration Reform and Immigrant Responsibility Act (IIRAIRA) significantly tightened rules that permitted undocumented immigrants to convert to legal status and also tightened immigration law in areas such as political asylum and deportation.

Fifth, in response to the September 11, 2001, terrorist attacks, the USA PATRIOT Act and the Enhanced Border Security and Visa Entry Reform Act tightened rules on the granting of visas to individuals from certain countries and enhanced the federal government's monitoring and detention authority over foreign nationals in the United States.

New U.S. Immigration Agencies

In a dramatic reorganization of the federal government, the Homeland Security Act of 2002 abolished the Immigration and Naturalization Service and transferred its immigration service and enforcement functions from the Department of Justice into a new Department of Homeland Security. The Customs Service, the Coast Guard, and parts of other agencies were also transferred into the new department.

The Department of Homeland Security, with regards to immigration, is organized as follows: The Bureau of Customs and Border Protection (BCBP) contains Customs and Immigration inspectors, who check the documents of travelers to the United States at air, sea, and land ports of entry; and Border Patrol agents, the uniformed agents who seek to prevent unlawful entry along the southern and northern border. The new Bureau of Immigration and Customs Enforcement (BICE) employs investigators, who attempt to find undocumented immigrants inside the United States, and Detention and Removal officers, who detain and seek to deport such individuals. The new Bureau of Citizenship and Immigration Services (BCIS) is where people go, or correspond with, to become U.S. citizens or obtain permission to work or extend their stay in the United States.

Following the terrorist attacks of September 11, 2001, the Department of Justice adopted several measures that did not require new legislation to be passed by Congress. Some of these measures created controversy and raised concerns about civil liberties. For example, FBI and INS agents detained for months more than 1,000 foreign nationals of Middle Eastern descent and refused to release the names of the individuals. It is alleged that the Department of Justice adopted tactics that discouraged the detainees from obtaining legal

A sample page of an immigrant visa application, which Dominican and other immigrants fill out and return to U.S. consular offices before gaining entry for permanent residence in the country.

U.S. Department of State
APPLICATION FOR IMMIGRANT VISA AND ALIEN REGISTRATION

OMB APPROVAL NO. 1405-0015
EXPIRES: 05/31/2004
ESTIMATED BURDEN: 1 HOUR*
(See Page 2)

PART I - BIOGRAPHIC DATA

INSTRUCTIONS: Complete one copy of this form for yourself and each member of your family, regardless of age, who will immigrate with you. Please print or type your answers to all questions. Mark questions that are Not Applicable with "N/A". If there is insufficient room on the form, answer on a separate sheet using the same numbers that appear on the form. Attach any additional sheets to this form.

WARNING: Any false statement or concealment of a material fact may result in your permanent exclusion from the United States.

This form (DS-230 PART I) is the first of two parts. This part, together with Form DS-230 PART II, constitutes the complete Application for Immigrant Visa and Alien Registration.

1. Family Name	First Name	Middle Name

2. Other Names Used or Aliases *(If married woman, give maiden name)*

3. Full Name in Native Alphabet *(If Roman letters not used)*

4. Date of Birth *(mm-dd-yyyy)*	5. Age	6. Place of Birth (City or town)	*(Province)*	*(Country)*

7. Nationality *(If dual national, give both)*	8. Gender	9. Marital Status
	☐ Male	☐ Single *(Never married)* ☐ Married ☐ Widowed ☐ Divorced ☐ Separated
	☐ Female	Including my present marriage, I have been married_____ times.

10. Permanent address in the United States where you intend to live, if known *(street address including zip code)*. Include the name of a person who currently lives there.

11. Address in the United States where you want your Permanent Resident Card *(Green Card)* mailed, if different from address in item #10 *(include the name of a person who currently lives there)*.

Telephone number:

Telephone number:

12. Your Present Occupation

13. Present Address *(Street Address) (City or Town) (Province) (Country)*

Telephone number: Home   Office

14. Name of Spouse *(Maiden or family name)*   First Name   Middle Name

Date *(mm-dd-yyyy)* and place of birth of spouse:

Address of spouse *(If different from your own)*:

Spouse's occupation: Date of marriage *(mm-dd-yyyy)*:

15. Father's Family Name	First Name	Middle Name

16. Father's Date of Birth *(mm-dd-yyyy)*	Place of Birth	Current Address	If deceased, give year of death

17. Mother's Family Name at Birth	First Name	Middle Name

18. Mother's Date of Birth *(mm-dd-yyyy)*	Place of Birth	Current Address	If deceased, give year of death

DS-230 Part I
05-2001

THIS FORM MAY BE OBTAINED FREE AT CONSULAR OFFICES OF THE UNITED STATES OF AMERICA
PREVIOUS EDITIONS OBSOLETE

Page 1 of 4

assistance. The Department of Justice also began requiring foreign nationals from primarily Muslim nations to be fingerprinted and questioned by immigration officers upon entry or if they have been living in the United States. Those involved in the September 11 attacks were not immigrants—people who become permanent residents with a right to stay in the United States—but holders of temporary visas, primarily visitor or tourist visas.

Immigration to the United States Today

Today, the annual rate of legal immigration is lower than that at earlier periods in U.S. history. For example, from 1901 to 1910 approximately 10.4 immigrants per 1,000 U.S. residents came to the United States. Today, the annual rate is about 3.5 immigrants per 1,000 U.S. residents. While the percentage of foreign-born people in the U.S. population has risen above 11 percent, it remains lower than the 13 percent or higher that prevailed in the country from 1860 to 1930. Still, as has been the case previously in U.S. history, some people argue that even legal immigration should be lowered. These people maintain that immigrants take jobs native-born Americans could fill and that U.S. population growth, which immigration contributes to, harms the environment. In 1996 Congress voted against efforts to reduce legal immigration.

Most immigrants (800,000 to one million annually) enter the United States legally. But over the years the undocumented (illegal) portion of the population has increased to about 2.8 percent of the U.S. population— approximately 8 million people in all.

Today, the legal immigration system in the United States contains many rules, permitting only individuals who fit into certain categories to immigrate—and in many cases only after waiting anywhere from 1 to 10 years or more, depending on the demand in that category. The system, representing a compromise among family, employment, and human rights concerns, has the following elements:

> A U.S. citizen may sponsor for immigration a spouse, parent, sibling, or minor or adult child.

> A lawful permanent resident (green card holder) may sponsor only a spouse or child.

> A foreign national may immigrate if he or she gains an employer sponsor.

> An individual who can show that he or she has a "well-founded fear of persecution" may come to the country as a refugee—or be allowed to stay as an asylee (someone who receives asylum).

Beyond these categories, essentially the only other way to immigrate is to apply for and receive one of the "diversity" visas, which are granted annually by lottery to those from "underrepresented" countries.

In 1996 changes to the law prohibited nearly all incoming immigrants from being eligible for federal public benefits, such as welfare, during their first five years in the country. Refugees were mostly excluded from these changes. In addition, families who sponsor relatives must sign an affidavit of support showing they can financially take care of an immigrant who falls on hard times.

A Short History of Canadian Immigration

In the 1800s, immigration into Canada was largely unrestricted. Farmers and artisans from England and Ireland made up a significant portion of 19th-century immigrants. England's Parliament passed laws that facilitated and encouraged the voyage to North America, particularly for the poor.

After the United States barred Chinese railroad workers from settling in the country, Canada encouraged the immigration of Chinese laborers to assist in the building

Lester Pearson, prime minister of Canada from 1963 to 1968, believed that immigrants were key to the country's economic growth. In 1966 the Canadian government introduced a statement stressing the importance of an open immigration policy.

of Canadian railways. Responding to the racial views of the time, the Canadian Parliament began charging a "head tax" for Chinese and South Asian (Indian) immigrants in 1885. The fee of $50—later raised to $500—was well beyond the means of laborers making one or two dollars a day. Later, the government sought additional ways to prohibit Asians from entering the country. For example, it decided to require a "continuous journey," meaning that immigrants to Canada had to travel from their country on a boat that made an uninterrupted passage. For immigrants or asylum seekers from Asia this was nearly impossible.

As the 20th century progressed, concerns about race led to further restrictions on immigration to Canada. These restrictions particularly hurt Jewish and other refugees seeking to flee persecution in Europe. Government statistics indicate that Canada accepted no more than 5,000 Jewish refugees before and during the Holocaust.

After World War II, Canada, like the United States, began accepting thousands of Europeans displaced by the war. Canada's laws were modified to accept these war refugees, as well as Hungarians fleeing Communist authorities after the crushing of the 1956 Hungarian Revolution.

The Immigration Act of 1952 in Canada allowed for a "tap on, tap off" approach to immigration, granting administrative authorities the power to allow more immigrants into the country in good economic times, and fewer in times of recession. The shortcoming of such an approach is that there is little evidence immigrants harm a national economy and much evidence they contribute to economic growth, particularly in the growth of the labor force.

In 1966 the government of Prime Minister Lester Pearson introduced a policy statement stressing how immigrants were key to Canada's economic growth. With Canada's relatively small population base, it became clear that in the absence of newcomers, the country would not be able to grow. The policy was introduced four years after Parliament enacted important legislation that eliminated Canada's own version of racially based national-origin quotas.

In 1967 a new law established a points system that awarded entry to potential immigrants using criteria based primarily on an individual's age, language ability, skills, education, family relationships, and job prospects.

The total points needed for entry of an immigrant is set by the Minister of Citizenship and Immigration Canada. The new law also established a category for humanitarian (refugee) entry.

The 1976 Immigration Act refined and expanded the possibility for entry under the points system, particularly for those seeking to sponsor family members. The act also expanded refugee and asylum law to comport with Canada's international obligations. The law established

A Literary Testament

The literature of Dominican American Julia Alvarez is a testament of the Dominican immigrant experience. Alvarez was born in New York City in 1950, but grew up in the Dominican Republic, her parents' homeland. She spent the first 10 years of her life on the island, until her father was implicated in a plan to overthrow dictator Rafael Trujillo and the family was forced to flee the country. They returned to Queens, where many of her experiences as a Dominican living in New York inspired her later writing.

She attended Connecticut College and graduated from Middlebury College in 1971, then obtained a master's degree from Syracuse University in 1975. She published her first book of poems, *Homecoming*, in 1984, and was awarded a National Endowment for the Arts fellowship in 1987. She returned to Middlebury College in 1988, this time as a professor of English. Alvarez's works have appeared in such publications as the *New Yorker*, the *New York Times Magazine*, and the *Kenyon Review*.

In her writings, Alvarez observes the radical cultural differences between her two homelands. Her first novel, *How the Garcia Girls Lost Their Accents*, is a collection of 15 intertwined stories covering 30 years of the lives of the Garcia sisters, who are forced to flee the Dominican Republic and grow up in the United States. Yolanda, one of the Garcia sisters, makes another appearance in a later novel titled *Yo!* Other works by Alvarez deal with the Dominican fight for independence and the immigrant struggle for a sense of identity.

Perhaps Alvarez's most well-known novel, *In The Time of the Butterflies*, was published in 1994 and is a fictional account of a true story involving four sisters who publicly opposed the Trujillo dictatorship.

Between 1960 and 1996, Joaquín Balaguer served as president of the Dominican Republic for three nonconsecutive terms. Early in his presidency he opened up the country's emigration, allowing tens of thousands of Dominicans to receive passports to travel abroad.

five basic categories for immigration into Canada: 1) family; 2) humanitarian; 3) independents (including skilled workers), who immigrate to Canada on their own; 4) assisted relatives; and 5) business immigrants (including investors, entrepreneurs, and the self-employed).

The new Immigration and Refugee Protection Act, which took effect June 28, 2002, made a series of modifications to existing Canadian immigration law. The act, and the regulations that followed, toughened rules on those seeking asylum and the process for removing people unlawfully in Canada.

The law modified the points system, adding greater flexibility for skilled immigrants and temporary workers to become permanent residents, and evaluating skilled

Many Dominican Americans own and manage bodegas like this one in Manhattan, New York City. Dominican bodegas are places where immigrants can find Caribbean food and Spanish-language newspapers.

workers on the weight of their transferable skills as well as those of their specific occupation. The legislation also made it easier for employers to have a labor shortage declared in an industry or sector, which would facilitate the entry of foreign workers in that industry or sector.

On family immigration, the act permitted parents to sponsor dependent children up to the age of 22 (previously 19 was the maximum age at which a child could be sponsored for immigration). The act also allowed partners in common-law arrangements, including same-sex partners, to be considered as family members for the purpose of immigration sponsorship. Along with these liberalizing measures, the act also included provisions to address perceived gaps in immigration-law enforcement.

Immigration from the Dominican Republic

Before the 1930s, immigration numbers from the Dominican Republic were low, but in succeeding decades migration has increased dramatically. As of the U.S. and Canadian census reports of 2000 and 2001, respectively, there are over 697,000 people from the Dominican Republic, or over 8 percent of the country's population, estimated to legally reside in North America. Although a majority of Dominican immigrants have settled in New York City, through the years many have gradually begun to venture out from the city to other locales along the East Coast.

Before Joaquín Balaguer served as president (1960–62, 1966–78, 1986–96), Rafael Trujillo had kept a tight rein on emigration from the Dominican Republic. Generally, only the wealthy members of Trujillo's inner circle were given the passports needed to travel abroad. After Trujillo was assassinated in 1961, the number of Dominicans applying for passports and visas increased dramatically, as did the number of Dominicans admitted into North America as permanent residents. Passports were handed out to nearly everyone who applied under Balaguer's rule. In 1959, a year during Trujillo's presidency, only 1,805 people of the nearly 20,000 who applied received a passport; by contrast, in 1969 all of the 63,695 people who requested a passport received one.

Throughout the 1970s, a decade of low sugar prices, and into the 1980s more and more Dominicans wished to escape poverty and migrate to the United States. Eventually, the numbers became staggering. In *A Continent of Islands*, author Mark Kurlansky surveys Dominican immigration during this period:

> By the late 1980s, the consulate in Santo Domingo was handling some 120,000 visa applications per year, which meant each officer had to process an average of thirteen cases every half hour. The case load was increasing by about 25 percent every year. After 1986 a steady decline of the Dominican economy made Dominicans one of the fastest-growing immigrant groups in the United States. By the 1990s there was no other country in the world with as high a percentage of its population legally immigrating to the United States.

During the second half of the 20th century, Dominican immigrants slowly established communities in the United States and Canada. The exiles of the Trujillo era were generally only middle- or upper-class Dominicans, and most decided to immigrate to Cuba before considering to settle in the United States. Later in the Trujillo presidency, many exiles made New York their final destination. They were typically political opponents who had either suffered economic losses or who had grown weary of the regime.

During the 1970s, most of the Dominicans deciding to emigrate were more representative of the general populace than the exiles of the Trujillo era. These migrants were primarily looking for better economic opportunities. With little or no income, many became desperate and were willing to risk their lives by taking illegal passage to nearby Puerto Rico. There, some Dominicans sought to secure false documents as Puerto Rican nationals. Because Puerto Rico is a U.S. commonwealth, these documents could possibly gain the migrants entrance into the United States or Canada.

Many Dominican immigrants use money transfer businesses like this one in Washington Heights, New York. A large portion of the wages that immigrants make finances businesses and improves living standards in the Dominican Republic.

In the late 1990s Dominican immigrants in general were more economically secure than before, perhaps a result of the recent stabilization of the Dominican government. These immigrants tended to be better educated than those still living in the homeland, and many brought professional expertise with them to their new communities. A large segment of this group has since heavily invested in small businesses. According to the INS, Dominicans make up a large segment of the self-employed among foreign-born immigrants in the country (7 percent), and the largest segment among all Hispanics in New York City.

Many Dominican small business owners run bodegas (corner grocery stores), the majority of which are located in the Dominican neighborhoods of New York City and other metropolitan areas. In fact, one study reported that about 70 percent of all bodegas in New York City are owned by Dominicans. Other successful businesses organized and operated by Dominicans are supermarkets, restaurants, discount phone services, beauty parlors, insurance and travel agencies, and car servicing.

Contributing to the Homeland

One of the more positive results of the investments of Dominican immigrants is the great amount of money they have sent home to relatives. Some of the wages immigrants make are used to finance domestic businesses, purchase land and housing, provide for Dominican churches, and generally improve the living standards of family members who have remained behind. Most working Dominicans consider it their obligation to send money back home. Those who do not send money are often chastised by fellow Dominicans living abroad.

According to a 2001 study by the Inter-American Bank for Development, Latin Americans return over $23 billion annually to their home countries (the study's results only reflect official bank transfers). Among Latin American countries the Dominican Republic ranks third in sums of money sent to the homeland from U.S.–based immigrants, with $1.9 billion sent back to family and friends in 2002, according to the U.S. Department of State.

During the mid-1970s, 85 percent of Dominican households from one village in the central region of Cibao had at least one family member living in New York. At that same time, remittances helped to spur the building of houses in migrants' home neighborhoods and villages, which in turn helped increase employment and spending. Through the 1990s and into the new century, remittances accounted for the second-largest source of foreign money coming into the Dominican Republic. Only the tourism industry garnered more money for the Dominican economy.

4 PROFILE OF THE DOMINICAN IMMIGRANT

Dominicans are one of the newest groups immigrating to North America today, and in many respects they are still carving out a niche for themselves in the United States and Canada. Naturally, Dominicans bring with them experiences and an economic background that helps shape their lives in North America.

The average Dominican immigrant leaves behind a life of few resources—some 40 percent of people born in the Dominican Republic live below the poverty level. In 2002 the average Dominican earned a monthly income of $450—an annual income of $5,400. The poor generally do not have access to the best schools, which means they often only speak their native language and are less likely to learn English. Those without a command of the language arrive into the United States and Canada at a distinct disadvantage.

Many Dominican immigrants, however, are at least familiar with the resettlement process, having already migrated within their own country. According to census figures, more than 25 percent of Dominicans live in a different province than the one in which they were born. At one point, nearly two-thirds of city residents and over half of those living in rural areas had migrated within the country at least once.

In the latter half of the 20th century, peasants, laborers,

◀A man rides a donkey down a country road to the town of Las Galeras. During the second half of the 20th century, many Dominicans from the countryside resettled in the country's cities, which underwent a population increase. After finding few opportunities there, some picked up again and moved to the United States and Canada.

and homeless people moved from the countryside into growing urban areas. These migrants became referred to as "Campunos." Immigrants to the United States have reflected this trend: nearly half of the more than 21,000 Dominican immigrants admitted to the United States in 2001 listed New York City as their intended residence. (Other metropolitan areas that ranked high that year were Miami and the small cities of New Jersey just outside New York.)

Campunos will typically leave their farming community to seek out new sources of income in non-agricultural

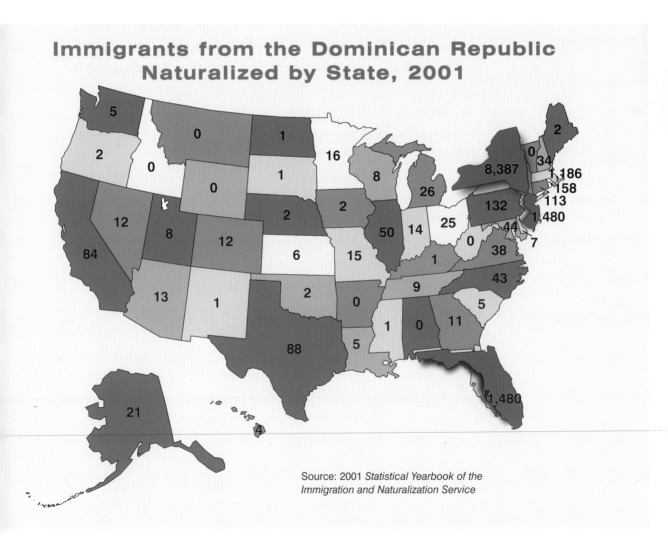

Immigrants from the Dominican Republic Naturalized by State, 2001

Source: 2001 *Statistical Yearbook of the Immigration and Naturalization Service*

occupations. Usually, they will go through a series of steps to accomplish this goal, acquiring experience in smaller cities before seeking out better-paying jobs in major urban areas. Campunos in general will earn a better living than those who do not migrate, since many seek training and higher education and end up with careers as teachers, skilled workers, and government officials. Often saddled with responsibilities to needy family members, Campunos may send a good portion of their earnings back home.

The Typical Immigrant

During the 1980s and 1990s, a gap widened between low-skilled Dominicans and professionals immigrating to North America. In the late 1990s and early years of the new century, this gap has continued to widen and prohibit the less advantaged from migrating. Currently, the most impoverished segment of the Dominican homeland population makes up the smallest segment of the Dominican immigrant population. In other words, the poorest Dominicans have virtually little or no chance of ever migrating to North America.

Of those who have the opportunity to migrate, a large segment arrives having received limited education. Many Dominicans are not initially prepared for the hardships of their new land, and once transplanted, they often find that they are under-skilled and thus forced to take manual-labor jobs. Dominicans who would otherwise be able to procure professional positions may be caught unaware of an ever-changing labor market that necessitates a full command of the English language.

The garment industry in the New York metropolitan area provides many manual-labor jobs, and employs a great number of Dominican women. These women typically work for companies that are not unionized, and

Many Latino workers—a large segment of them Dominicans—work in garment factories like this one in New York City. Work conditions are poor in many factories, with low wages, no workmen's compensation, and little job security.

they are often paid in cash. They have virtually no job protection or benefits, and their wages are lower than those of most U.S. citizens. Dominicans who are not employed in the garment industry may find other factory work or jobs in restaurants and grocery stores.

A large number of Dominican immigrants work in the service sector, which generally entails small workplaces. It is common for Dominican immigrants to purchase and run small businesses, as they typically require few employees, little space to operate, and low overhead costs. These businesses often include taxicab services, beauty salons, travel services, and discount phone services to the Dominican Republic.

Many Dominicans immigrants work to fulfill responsibilities to relatives back home, and they may also have obligations to family members in North America who have sponsored them. Sponsors immediately try to find work for newcomers and typically welcome them into their homes. Extended family households often include Dominicans from two, three, and even four families. Once they have achieved some financial independence, immigrants are usually expected to repay family members for their generosity.

In the late 1990s the trend of multiple families living in one home appeared to be waning. This decline perhaps could be attributed to the frequent conflicts that arise in such a living situation. Nevertheless, today very few Dominicans are able to arrive into North America on their own. Nearly all immigrants rely on some type of family or peer support wherever they are settling.

Oscar de la Renta

Fashion designer Oscar de la Renta is one of the most internationally famous Dominican immigrants to North America. Born on July 22, 1932, in Santo Domingo, de la Renta was the only boy among seven children in a middle-class family. In 1950 he graduated from a teacher-training course at the national university in Santo Domingo. After finishing his studies he left for Madrid, Spain, to study painting at the Academy of San Fernando.

Soon, de la Renta was sketching designs for some of Spain's most famous clothing designers and landing an apprenticeship with top fashion magnate Cristobal Balenciaga. He later left to become a fashion design assistant at Lanvin in Paris. In 1963 de la Renta arrived in New York City to begin designing for Elizabeth Arden. Just two years later he was sketching works for his own label. Today, Oscar de la Renta has a full line of fashion wear and accessories, including bags, belts, jewelry, scarves, shoes, sportswear, sleepwear, furniture, and fragrances. In 1977 he introduced his first perfume product, "Oscar," and it quickly became a bestseller in over 70 countries.

In 1971 de la Renta became a U.S. citizen. In the years since then, he has divided his time between his home in New York and his home in the resort town of Punta Cana in the Dominican Republic. In keeping loyal to his roots, he has founded schools and day care centers in the Dominican Republic that serve more than 1,500 children. De la Renta has received awards from many countries, including the Order of Juan Pablo Duarte, an award that the Dominican government gives for distinguished service.

Dominican Enclaves

The Dominican culture is one of strong-knit family ties that can keep extended families together even in a vast new land like the United States. As a result of this closeness, Dominicans have settled together in specific locales in North America such as New York City and the metropolitan areas of northern New Jersey.

New York City hosts the largest Dominican population outside the island. Many Dominicans have come to treasure New York and the opportunities it offers, often reciting the popular folk saying, "He who dies without seeing New York dies blind." Dominican immigrants flocked to the city primarily during the latter third of the 20th century. Initially, most Dominicans settled in the Lower East Side of Manhattan, just as other immigrants before them had done, enjoying its employment opportunities and cheap living conditions.

But as Dominicans became more familiar with Manhattan, they began to branch out to other areas of the city. Many Dominican immigrants settled in Corona in the borough of Queens and Rockville Center on Long Island. Washington Heights in Upper Manhattan became the most Dominicanized of any neighborhood in New York. Locals even named it Quisqueya Heights after the precolonial name for the homeland.

Another section in New York City that is heavily populated by Dominicans is Highbridge, located in the borough of the Bronx. In this neighborhood rental fees for apartments are as high as those in the more-established Washington Heights. Dominicans began to move into Highbridge in the mid-1990s. In fact, of the 8,092 immigrants who moved to Highbridge between 1995 and 1996, 5,722 were Dominicans, according to a report by the New York City Department of City Planning statistics service.

The influx of Dominicans to Highbridge's main corner (Odgen Avenue and 161st Street) helped create a resurgence in business. The six-block business sector now is home to salons, bodegas, and travel agencies—the majority of which are run by Dominican immigrants.

When immigrants are immersed among their own people in a new and strange environment, they can more easily adapt to their new lifestyle. For this reason, Dominican immigrants have tended to congregate in large communities in New York City and other metropolitan areas. In communities where familiar customs and lifestyles are found, new surroundings appear less foreign and foreboding to the Dominican immigrant, and the transition to North American life a little less daunting.

Visitors can observe Dominican unity just by walking down the street of an immigrant community. They will spot Dominican restaurants, where owners often hire immigrants who are proficient in Spanish as well as English. Local businesses often place signs in their windows that read "*Se Habla Español*" to announce that they welcome and can communicate with Dominican customers and clients. As another form of welcome, owners of local eateries or grocery stores will put stickers of the Dominican flag in their windows, and often restaurant owners will display full-size Dominican flags with American or Canadian flags above their establishments.

It is also common for visitors to Dominican communities to hear residents speaking Spanish with the

Hoy, which is published in New York, and other Spanish-language newspapers are commonly found in major U.S. cities. Many Dominican newcomers stay connected with the homeland culture through reading these newspapers, eating at Dominican restaurants, and shopping at Dominican stores.

Dominican dialect. This is one major way Dominicans connect with each other and remember the homeland. They also read Spanish-language newspapers like *El Diario*, which is published in New York, and in major U.S. and Canadian cities they may buy periodicals like *El Tiempo*, *El Nacíonal*, *El Popular*, and *El Caribe*. These papers helps keep newcomers informed about developments in their new communities as well as the ones back on the island.

Finally, consulate offices help new Dominican immigrants feel acclimated to their new homes. They offer immigrants assistance with handling and preparing official forms and adjusting to life in the United States or Canada. There are fifteen Dominican consulate offices in the United States, three in Puerto Rico, and three in Canada (in Montreal, Ottawa, and Toronto).

Festivals and Culture

Celebrating festivals is one of the most popular ways Dominican newcomers stay connected with their cultural roots. The largest of these festivals is the annual Dominican Day Parade, celebrated in August. One of Manhattan's most widely attended events, the parade has been celebrated annually since 1982. In 2002 New York City Mayor Michael Bloomberg marched alongside nearly 200,000 New Yorkers down Manhattan's streets in the parade.

Dominican food can be found throughout communities in groceries and on dinner tables. Favorite dishes reflecting the island's heritage are *empanadas* (meat or fruit-filled tortillas) and *plantinos* (fried, sliced, and flattened bananas); a favorite treat is *frío-frío* (snow cone). Music genres that are popular in the Dominican neighborhoods are *bachata* (romantic guitar music), merengue (traditional Dominican dance music), and

New York City Mayor Michael Bloomberg shakes hands with attendants of the annual Dominican Day Parade in August 2003. The parade is one of the city's most widely attended events.

salsa (Latin dance music).

Holidays are an important part of Dominican life in North America. Major days of celebration besides Christmas and Easter include the Day of the Virgin of Altagracia (High Grace), the birthday of Dominican founding father Juan Pablo Duarte, Dominican Independence Day, Independence Restoration Day, Day of the Virgin of Mercedes, and Constitution Day, recognized on November 6.

For many Dominican immigrants, commitments to the Catholic Church are second in importance only to commitments to the family and the home. Church services are a big part of Dominican life, and in immigrant communities they may be held in both English and Spanish. Dominicans often attend church during the weekdays, and it is traditional to stop in the afternoon by a local church to light a candle and say a prayer. Many Dominican houses and businesses also have small shrines to the Virgin Mary or Catholic saints in their homes and offices. Flowers, candles, and offerings

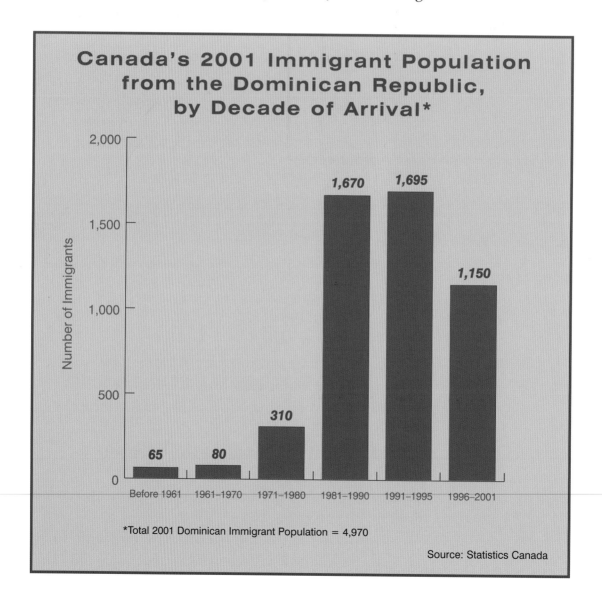

Canada's 2001 Immigrant Population from the Dominican Republic, by Decade of Arrival*

*Total 2001 Dominican Immigrant Population = 4,970

Source: Statistics Canada

such as food and wines are often placed around these shrines. Many Dominicans also will wear religious ornaments on their clothing, or carry rosaries or wear chains with lockets that contain images of Christ or the Virgin Mary.

Loyalty to the Homeland

Despite the opportunities that Dominican immigrants have to reconnect with their culture in New York and other cities, the loyalty they have to their homeland may prevent them from ever completely assimilating in their new communities. One popular Dominican expression is *"Mi patria, mi tierra, mi país"* (My fatherland, my land, my country). The loyalty that this expression imparts remains with many Dominican immigrants. And because the Dominican Republic is only a three-hour plane ride away from New York, it is relatively easy for immigrants to feel that home is never too far away.

As a result of the circumstances that newcomers face, many do not look to permanently settle or assimilate in the United States. Even those who apply to become U.S. citizens may someday decide to return to their family in the Dominican Republic. This has been an option since 1994, when an amendment to the Dominican Republic's constitution allowed emigrants to receive dual citizenship. After Leonel Fernández took office in 1996, the U.S.–educated president urged Dominicans residing in the United States to apply for citizenship and enjoy the privileges that come with it. At the same time, he encouraged Dominican immigrants wishing to return to the country to do so, and if they had saved money in the United States, to reinvest it in the Dominican economy.

6 SMUGGLING AND THE TRIALS OF THE WORKPLACE

Two major problems facing the Dominican immigrant community are poverty and the dangers of illegal migration. In many cases these problems are interrelated. For example, many Dominicans who are too frustrated with the poverty of the homeland feel they cannot endure the slow process of obtaining a visa, or they cannot afford the fees for legal passage to North America. As an alternative, they choose to either be smuggled into Puerto Rico first or directly into the United States, courses of action that present unforeseen dangers and problems. Those undocumented Dominicans who safely migrate and settle in the United States still may remain poor because they can only take jobs that offer very low wages and little or no stability.

More than one-third of New York–based Dominicans live below the poverty level. There is a high level of unemployment among this group, as well as a high rate of individuals receiving public assistance, more than any other Hispanic or Latino group. And although Dominicans who immigrate to North America today are better trained and educated than many of their predecessors, over 69 percent of the employed still work as basic laborers, according to the 2001 *Statistical Yearbook of the Immigration and Naturalization Service*.

Dominican immigrants make up a large segment of

◄ U.S. Coast Guard officers prepare to process Dominican migrants who were discovered on a sailboat off the Florida Keys, 1986. There are many dangers facing Dominicans who try to illegally migrate, and those who safely arrive to the United States without legal status may still face difficulties.

Fighting Crime in Washington Heights

In recent years, problems with drug and gang activity have plagued the Washington Heights neighborhood, with a number of Dominican youth falling into a cycle of drugs, crime, and gang violence. For law-abiding immigrants, this adds an element of danger that was neither welcomed nor expected in their new land.

Many immigrant parents have tried to address the youth crime problem by claiming a leadership role in the community. In the 1990s, Dominican parents living in Washington Heights worked hard to secure a seat on the local school board, where Dominican children represented the majority of youngsters in that district. Their success inspired a more concerted effort by Dominicans to seek political positions within New York City. Manhattan, in particular, provides young immigrants with a wide array of Dominican student organizations and outreach programs, as well as a specialized program in Dominican Studies at the City University of New York.

workers in the New York City garment industry—about 15 percent in 2002. The majority of these workers are women. This occupation has proved to be fruitful and has provided modest advancements in position and salary for some Dominican women and men, but many have not advanced at all. Some of these workers find themselves transferred to smaller operations when the big companies close down. These firms usually provide immigrant workers with less pay and no benefits like social security, health insurance, or workmen's compensation.

Immigrants forced to work for smaller companies may face dramatic life changes, especially if they were previously employed by a unionized factory and were used to being provided with health insurance and other standard benefits. Some smaller garment shops also close during a season known as "down time," from September to January, which can put additional economic hardships on Dominican immigrants who cannot find work during these months.

As a consequence of living in a country with different work environments, many family and gender roles within Dominican immigrant families change. The patriarchal system of the Dominican Republic is more prevalent than it is in North America, with males as the traditional head of the household making the money and parenting decisions. More Dominican women in North America procure greater control over household budgets than in the homeland. This new empowerment factored into the increase in single-parent households headed by women during the late 1990s.

The U.S. Coast Guard Cutter *Monomoy* is a patrol boat that, along with tracking down drug smugglers, picks up migrants at sea. The Coast Guard has reported picking up over 4,000 Dominicans every year since the mid-1990s.

The Dangers of Smuggling

In seeking to gain entry into the United States or
Canada, Dominican immigrants and immigrants from
other countries face similar problems. A common solu-
tion for some is to try to illegally enter North America
by using forged papers or smugglers. Immigrant smuggling has been a multi-billion dollar since the end of the
1990s, and shows no signs of slowing down in the new
century.

Undocumented Dominicans typically pay anywhere
from $500 to $1,200 to have themselves or their relatives smuggled out of the Dominican Republic and into
the U.S. territory of Puerto Rico. The Dominican
Republic, Cuba, and Haiti are the source countries of
the majority of undocumented migrants found at sea by
the U.S. Coast Guard.

Global Reach, a program established by the INS
(Immigration and Naturalization Services) in 2001,
helped to combat illegal smuggling of aliens into the
United States. One of the main reasons the INS devel-
oped this program was to try to lower instances of death
or serious injury, as well as to curb the trafficking of
women and children for illicit activities.

Since the mid-1990s the number of Dominicans being
smuggled illegally onto North American soil has grown
steadily. The U.S. Coast Guard has reported picking up
some 4,000 or more Dominicans annually. Most of these
migrants are poor Dominicans who hire smugglers to
take them by boat on the 18-hour-long ride to Puerto
Rico. Once established in that island community, these
Dominicans often find it easier to get into the United
States. The U.S. Coast Guard routinely picks up
Dominicans and people from other islands who are
attempting to cross borders illegally, as well as those
who die during the journey.

In January 2000 a sailboat on the Mona Passage, a strait connecting the Caribbean Sea and the Atlantic Ocean, capsized and dozens of Dominicans died. The Dominican navy assisted the U.S. Coast Guard after 15 Dominicans swam ashore and reported the incident to the authorities. Authorities estimate that hundreds of illegal migrants drown each year in the Mona Passage and their bodies are never recovered.

In late November 2002, the U.S. Coast Guard apprehended four boats carrying 172 undocumented Dominican immigrants in waters near the United States. At around the same time another boat filled to capacity with Dominicans flipped over en route to Puerto Rico. In that month alone, the U.S. Coast Guard reported repatriating 441 migrants back to the Dominican Republic.

7 THE FUTURE

Although opportunities are available to Dominicans who immigrate to North America in the 21st century, immigration laws limit the number of people from this island nation able to migrate annually.

While immigration numbers from the Dominican Republic were high in the early 1990s (45,420 in 1993 and 51,189 in 1994), by the end of the decade the annual number of Dominicans crossing the Caribbean waters dropped to a low of under 18,000, according to the 2000 *Statistical Yearbook of the Immigration and Naturalization Service.*

Radhamés Peguero, Executive Director of the Dominican American National Foundation (DANF), explains that the reason for the drop in the number of Dominicans migrating to North America—primarily to New York City and other large metropolitan areas—has nothing to do with the people's desire, but with paperwork overload:

> Because of changes in the immigration laws of 1996, the paperwork required to bring Dominicans into North America—primarily the United States, has become a problem. This process can often take four or five years, and our community does not yet have the resources (money) available to help speed up the process. Because the system is overloaded with so many people desiring to migrate here, there is a constant backlog.

The totals of Dominican immigrants to the United States were 21,256 in 2001 and 22,474 in 2002. Peguero predicts

◀ Latino students at an elementary school in Tyler, Texas, recite the Pledge of Allegiance during a memorial service for victims of the September 2001 attacks. Young Dominican newcomers to the United States join a steadily growing Latino immigrant population, of which 35 percent are under the age of 18.

that on average about 23,000 will be able to migrate annually through the middle of the 21st century unless the current laws are modified.

In 2003 the Dominican Republic witnessed several problems in the homeland that has helped to fuel the desire to migrate north. There was persistent inflation, and damaging power losses occurred for up to 20 hours at a time. An unstable peso against the U.S. dollar has made the situations of some Dominicans even more precarious. As a result of these stressful conditions, there were an increasing number of visa and residency applications.

Continuing Challenges

Although in the 21st century there are generally better conditions for immigrants to North America, many Dominicans will continue to struggle with social, economic, and domestic challenges. Pressures from relatives

New York City, home to the immigrant landmark the Statue of Liberty, remains the final destination for the majority of Dominican newcomers. In Manhattan alone, one-third of the foreign-born population is from the Dominican Republic.

and friends back home and in North America will continue to plague new arrivals, often making assimilation difficult. In addition, some Dominicans may continue to protest that the North American media do not portray an accurate picture of their community. Although heralded as the birthplace of baseball heroes, the Dominican Republic also is often misrepresented as a producer of drug dealers and thugs who thrive on the streets of New York City. These stereotypes can sit poorly in the minds of Dominican newcomers, and may help fuel animosity between immigrants and American and Canadian citizens in the years ahead.

Despite the persistence of the stereotypes, New York City continues to be the place of choice for Dominicans to settle, as well as for other peoples of the Caribbean. According to the INS, during the 1990s about 17 percent of immigrants intending to settle in New York City were Dominicans. In the borough of the Bronx alone, 60 percent of the foreign-born populace was from the Caribbean, with 37 percent from the Dominican Republic, while over one-third of the foreign-born population in Manhattan was from the island nation. Queens is home to the largest segment of Dominicans anywhere in the New York City area. Overall, this area of the United States has long been seen as a place of opportunity and a chance for a better life among Dominican immigrants.

Economically, many Dominican immigrants hold a precarious position within their new societies, as the demand for basic laborers and high-level professionals increases. Those without the professional or language skills, or the opportunity to obtain these skills, will be challenged to find steady employment.

Among the Hispanic community as a whole, Dominicans show different levels of success than do groups like

Mexican Americans and Puerto Ricans. This inequality between the groups will not necessarily persist, especially if more members of the Dominican communities became involved in upper levels of management in the workplace. Groups that were disadvantaged, like Mexican and Cuban Americans, have addressed some of their problems by obtaining more leadership roles.

Finding Success

Determining one's place somewhere between the roots of the homeland and the new opportunity offered in the United States remains an important objective for many Dominicans. Wealthy immigrants will most likely move out of a poor neighborhood, which may convince their friends that they have forgotten where they came from. However, the upward mobility of Dominican Americans remains important for the overall success of the Dominican community. Successful immigrants can claim effective roles in public office and serve the many interests of the Dominican community.

Dominican women comprise one group of the immigrant population that has experienced great change. They are more likely to want to stay in either the United States or Canada than male immigrants, and are more likely to have jobs and contribute significantly to the household than they would working in the Dominican Republic. This newly found empowerment has given rise to many women living as single parents and choosing not to return to the Dominican Republic. They are also more likely to have a chance for a better education and to attain U.S. citizenship.

Serving as examples of this empowerment are service organizations like the Dominican Women's Development Center in Washington Heights. Established in 1988 by a group of professional Dominican women, the center's projects include running a family day care center and training program for the community and seeking grants and funds from the government and other organizations to help meet the needs of Dominican New Yorkers.

Dominicans in the 21st century are living in a country whose democratic principles are constantly being strengthened and reformed. The primary problem appears to be a failure to implement certain economic reforms, which threatens to keep poverty a stark reality

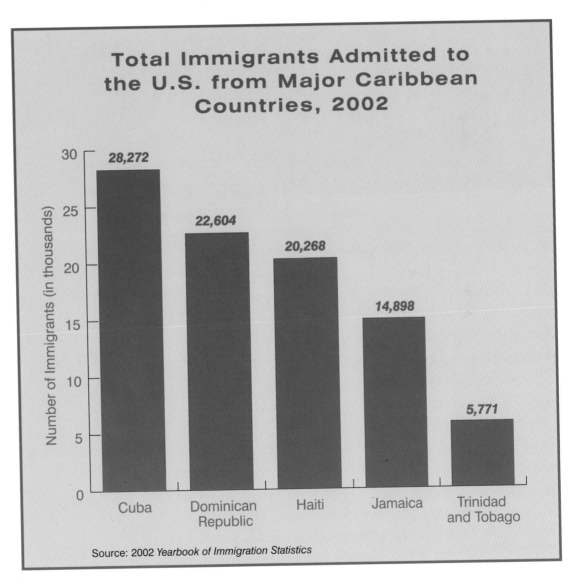

Total Immigrants Admitted to the U.S. from Major Caribbean Countries, 2002

Number of Immigrants (in thousands)

- Cuba: 28,272
- Dominican Republic: 22,604
- Haiti: 20,268
- Jamaica: 14,898
- Trinidad and Tobago: 5,771

Source: 2002 *Yearbook of Immigration Statistics*

The newest generation of Dominicans in North America will likely not feel the connection to the island country that first-generation Dominicans do, but they do have a greater chance of assimilating into North American culture.

for Dominicans. Those with the option to immigrate are presented with an attractive exit out of the country: the Dominican Republic's geographic proximity to North America allows emigrants opportunities not available to other nations in the developing world.

One thing is certain: those Dominicans who immigrate to North America know they may gain a better life for themselves and their families, and that they are leaving a life of perceived or real hopelessness. Absent a change in U.S. law or a dramatic improvement of the Dominican economy, approximately 200,000 people from the Dominican Republic will immigrate to the United States between 2002 and 2010. These numbers will contribute to the country's ever-growing Latino population.

As more and more children are born in North America to immigrant Dominican parents, the United States and Canada will see a new generation of Dominicans emerge. These children will not have the same feelings for the "old country" as their parents do. They will feel more in tune with the country in which they were born and raised, and may not feel a need to even visit the Dominican Republic until they are older, let alone understand the sacrifices their parents made for them. In some respects, these children may find more in common with their American or Canadian friends than they will with Dominicans living in the homeland.

Dominicans are a people who can clearly adapt well to change and to grow and learn from their new surroundings. Their love of family and proven success as business owners have given them a place among the many ethnic communities that help make up American and Canadian society in the 21st century.

FAMOUS DOMINICAN AMERICAN/CANADIANS

Josefina Báez (1960–), teacher, playwright, dancer, and actress who has appeared in theaters worldwide. In 1986 she founded and became director of Latinarte (1986), an art troupe that promotes the artistic expression of Latinas and Dominican women. She also teaches acting and creative writing to children and teens in New York City schools with large Dominican populations.

Junot Diaz (1968–), fiction writer best known for his *Negocios* (*Drown*), a short story collection published in 1996. His writings, some of which reflect the experiences of Dominican immigrants, have appeared in the *Paris Review* and the *New Yorker*, as well as in anthologies of Latin American literature.

Rhina Espaillat (1932–), high school English teacher, poet, and prose writer of English and Spanish works who moved to the United States from the Dominican Republic when she was seven years old. Her works have appeared in *The American Scholar* and some two dozen poetry anthologies. She was the youngest individual ever to be inducted into the Poetry Society of America.

Mary Joe Fernández (1971–), one of the top women tennis players of the United States in the 1990s. She migrated with her parents in 1972, settling in Miami, Florida. While going to high school she participated in four Grand Slam tournaments, playing at Wimbledon her sophomore year. At both the 1992 Olympic Games in Spain and the 1996 Atlanta games, she and her Puerto Rican partner, Gigi Fernández (no relation), won the gold medal in women's doubles for the United States.

Vladimir Guerrero (1976–), Montreal Expos outfielder and one of the top major league baseball players in North America in the late 1990s. He is one of only four players (with Joe DiMaggio, Ted Williams, and Jimmie Foxx) who had 30 home runs, 100 RBIs, and a .300 batting average in three consecutive years before age 25.

Pedro Martinez (1971–), professional baseball player who has played for the Los Angeles Dodgers, the Montreal Expos, and the Boston Red Sox. After making his major-league debut in 1992, he went on to win the Cy Young Award three times, and in 2003 pitched in the American League championship series.

FAMOUS DOMINICAN AMERICAN/CANADIANS

Ilka Tanya Payan (1943–96), writer and actor whose work has appeared in Spanish-language newspapers and Hispanic theaters. She also starred with Raul Julia in the HBO movie *Florida Straits* and played a leading role on the television series *Angelica, Mi Vida*, one of the first Spanish-language soap operas to air in the United States. At the time of her death from AIDS in 1996, she was an activist for AIDS awareness.

Manny Ramirez (1972–), professional baseball player who has played for the Cleveland Indians and the Boston Red Sox. He won the Silver Slugger award three years in a row and is a six-time All-Star player.

Alfonso Soriano (1978–), major league baseball player for the New York Yankees, which he helped lead to win the American League Championship in 2003. In 2002 he became the first second baseman to hit 30 home runs and steal 30 bases in the same season.

FURTHER READING

Austerlitz, Paul. *Dominican Music and Dominican Identity*. Philadelphia: Temple University Press, 1997.

Bailey, Benjamin H. *Language, Race, and Negotiation of Identity: A Study of Dominican Americans.* New York: LFB Scholarly Publishing, 2002.

Bandon, Alexandra. *Dominican Americans.* Parsippany, N.J.: New Discovery Books, 1995.

Foley, Erin. *Cultures of the World: The Dominican Republic*. New York: Marshall Cavendish, 1995.

Georges, Eugenia. *The Making of a Transnational Community: Migration, Development, and Cultural Change in the Dominican Republic.* New York: Columbia University Press, 1990.

Grasmuck, Sherri, and Patricia R. Pessar. *Between Two Islands: Dominican International Migration.* Berkeley, Calif.: University of California Press, 1991.

Hernández, Ramona, and Silvio Torres-Saillant. *Dominican Americans.* Westport, Conn.: Greenwood Press, 1996.

———. "Dominicans in New York: Men, Women, and Prospects," in *Latinos in New York*, ed. Gabriel Haslip-Viera. Notre Dame, Ind.: University of Notre Dame Press, 1996.

Hintz, Martin. *Haiti: Enchantment of the World*. New York: Children's Press, 1998.

Klein, Alan M. *Sugarball: The American Game, the Dominican Dream.* New Haven, Conn.: Yale University Press, 1991.

Kurlansky, Mark. *A Continent of Islands: Searching for the Caribbean*. Reading, Mass.: Addison-Wesley, 1992.

Pacini Hernandez, Deborah. *Bachata: A Social History of a Dominican Popular Music*. Philadelphia: Temple University Press, 1995.

Rogers, Luna, and Barbara Radcliffe. *The Dominican Republic.* New York: Children's Press, 1999.

FURTHER READING

Rogozinski, Jan. *A Brief History of the Caribbean.* New York: Facts on File, 1999.

Rohter, Larry. "Fewer Immigrant Benefits Do Not Faze Dominicans." *New York Times*, Oct. 12, 1996.

Wendel, Tim. *The New Face of Baseball*. New York: HarperCollins, 2003.

INTERNET RESOURCES

http://www.bcis.gov

The website of the Bureau of Citizenship and Immigration Services explains the various functions of the organization and provides specific information on immigration policy.

http://www.canadianhistory.ca/iv/main.html

This site contains an excellent history of immigration to Canada from the 1800s to the present.

www.amcham.org.do/english/

This site of the American Chamber of Commerce in the Dominican Republic provides information on American investments and firms in the Dominican Republic.

http://www.ccny.cuny.edu/dsi/index.html

The Dominican Studies Institute website is a source of information on Dominican life in the United States.

http://www.dr1.com

The Dominican Republic News and Travel Information Service provides daily coverage of the Dominican Republic and the Caribbean and offers other useful links to related web sites.

GLOSSARY

bodega—a small, neighborhood grocery store that can be found in Dominican communities in North America.

buscones **(boo-SCONE-ehs)**—the name for self-proposed agents who scout for young baseball prospects in hopes of securing them a major league baseball contract.

Campuno—a term used by Dominicans for migrants who have moved from the countryside into growing urban areas.

consulate—an office of a government representative appointed to a foreign country to serve the interests of its citizens.

junta—a small group of people assembled for a common goal; a traditional Dominican cooperative work group consisting of friends and relatives.

lawful permanent resident—a non-citizen legally residing in the United States.

mulatto—a term used to denote a person of mixed white and black ancestry.

Quisqueya—the original Spanish name for the Dominican Republic, as called by her original inhabitants, the Taino Indians.

repatriation—the return of a foreign national to his or her country of origin.

remittance—the act of sending money back to relatives or friends living in a country of birth.

transnationalism—the ability of immigrants to hold on to their native identities and customs while establishing a new home in a foreign land.

INDEX

Numbers in ***bold italic*** refer to captions.

INDEX

CONTRIBUTORS

SENATOR EDWARD M. KENNEDY has represented Massachusetts in the United States Senate for more than forty years. Kennedy serves on the Senate Judiciary Committee, where he is the senior Democrat on the Immigration Subcommittee. He currently is the ranking member on the Health, Education, Labor and Pensions Committee in the Senate, and also serves on the Armed Services Committee, where he is a member of the Senate Arms Control Observer Group. He is also a member of the Congressional Friends of Ireland and a trustee of the John F. Kennedy Center for the Performing Arts.

Throughout his career, Kennedy has fought for issues that benefit the citizens of Massachusetts and the nation, including the effort to bring quality health care to every American, education reform, raising the minimum wage, defending the rights of workers and their families, strengthening the civil rights laws, assisting individuals with disabilities, fighting for cleaner water and cleaner air, and protecting and strengthening Social Security and Medicare for senior citizens.

Kennedy is the youngest of nine children of Joseph P. and Rose Fitzgerald Kennedy, and is a graduate of Harvard University and the University of Virginia Law School. His home is in Hyannis Port, Massachusetts, where he lives with his wife, Victoria Reggie Kennedy, and children, Curran and Caroline. He also has three grown children, Kara, Edward Jr., and Patrick, and four grandchildren.

Senior consulting editor STUART ANDERSON served as Executive Associate Commissioner for Policy and Planning and Counselor to the Commissioner at the Immigration and Naturalization Service from August 2001 until January 2003. He spent four and a half years on Capitol Hill on the Senate Immigration Subcommittee, first for Senator Spencer Abraham and then as Staff Director of the subcommittee for Senator Sam Brownback. Prior to that, he was Director of Trade and Immigration Studies at the Cato Institute in Washington, D.C., where he produced reports on the history of immigrants in the military and the role of immigrants in high technology. He currently serves as Executive Director of the National Foundation for American Policy, a nonpartisan public policy research organization focused on trade, immigration, and international relations. He has an M.A. from Georgetown University and a B.A. in Political Science from Drew University. His articles have appeared in such publications as the *Wall Street Journal*, *New York Times*, and *Los Angeles Times*.

MARIAN L. SMITH served as the senior historian of the U.S. Immigration and Naturalization Service (INS) from 1988 to 2003, and is currently the immigration and naturalization historian within the Department of Homeland Security in Washington, D.C. She studies, publishes, and speaks on the history of the immigration agency and is active in management of official 20th-century immigration records.

PETER HAMMERSCHMIDT is the First Secretary (Financial and Military Affairs) for the Permanent Mission of Canada to the United Nations. Before taking this position, he was a ministerial speechwriter and policy specialist for the Department of National Defence in Ottawa. Prior to joining the public service, he served as the Publications

CONTRIBUTORS

Director for the Canadian Institute of Strategic Studies in Toronto. He has a B.A. (Honours) in Political Studies from Queen's University, and an MScEcon in Strategic Studies from the University of Wales, Aberystwyth. He currently lives in New York, where in his spare time he operates a freelance editing and writing service.

Manuscript reviewer ESTHER OLAVARRIA serves as General Counsel to Senator Edward M. Kennedy, ranking Democrat on the U.S. Senate Judiciary Committee, Subcommittee on Immigration. She is Senator Kennedy's primary advisor on immigration, nationality, and refugee legislation and policies. Previously, she practiced immigration law in Miami, Florida, working at several non-profit organizations. She cofounded the Florida Immigrant Advocacy Center and served as managing attorney, supervising the direct service work of the organization and assisting in the advocacy work. She also worked at Legal Services of Greater Miami, as the directing attorney of the American Immigration Lawyers Association Pro Bono Project, and at the Haitian Refugee Center, as a staff attorney. She clerked for a Florida state appellate court after graduating from the University of Florida Law School. She was born in Havana, Cuba, and raised in Florida.

Reviewer JANICE V. KAGUYUTAN is Senator Edward M. Kennedy's advisor on immigration, nationality, and refugee legislation and policies. Prior to working on Capitol Hill, Ms. Kaguyutan was a staff attorney at the NOW Legal Defense and Education Fund's Immigrant Women Program. Ms. Kaguyutan has written and trained extensively on the rights of immigrant victims of domestic violence, sexual assault, and human trafficking. Her previous work includes representing battered immigrant women in civil protection order, child support, divorce, and custody hearings, as well as representing immigrants before the Immigration and Naturalization Service on a variety of immigration matters.

KIMBERLY A. RINKER is a freelance author and editor living in Chicago. A graduate of Ohio State University with a B.A. in Journalism, she spent one year living and working in Switzerland. Her works have appeared in the *Chicago Tribune, Pompano Pelican, Hoof Beats, Prepared Foods, Sports Eye, Police Magazine, Inside Lincoln Park, Illinois Racing News, Avenue M,* and *Produce Business.* She is also the author of *An Adventure Guide to Switzerland.*

PICTURE CREDITS